BOOMERANG

PROUDLY AUSTRALIAN

D0249701

Published by Hinkler Books Pty Ltd
45–55 Fairchild Street
Heatherton Victoria 3202 Australia
www.hinkler.com.au

© Hinkler Books Pty Ltd 2013

Author: Lisa Regan
Cover Design: Sam Grimmer
Illustrations & typesetting: MPS Limited
Prepress: Graphic Print Group

Images © Dreamstime.com: Boomerang flying boy beach (p. 5)
© chrisvanlennepphotodotcom; Aboriginal Boomerang Isolated
© Stocksolutions.

Images © Fotolia.com: Wurfholz, Bumerangwerfer © Klaus Eppele;
Boomerang © Galyna Andrushko.

Images © Shutterstock.com: Mulga (tree) © Ashley Whitworth; Man with
boomerang in evening © Kesu; Boomerang over a blue sky © Gavran333;
Flowering of a mimosa/Silver Wattle tree © Flik47; Aboriginal traditional
boomerang © Mark Ditcham; Boomerang © bepsy; Brown boomerang
on overgrown sandy beach © Zurbagan; A man throws a frisbee in
the ocean © Ramon grosso dolarea; Wooden boomerang isolated
© RusGri, Australian boomerang isolated © ChaosMaker.

ISBN: 978 1 7435 2912 6

Printed and bound in China

Contents

Come back!

Congratulations! You are now the proud owner of a boomerang. You should probably prepare for the worst. It is highly likely that while reading this book and putting its advice into practice, several things will happen:

- You will test your own patience to its very limits.
- Your blood pressure will rise considerably.
- You will become physically exhausted.
- You will become totally and utterly hooked on throwing things in the hope that you can make them come back to you!

Sounds like your idea of fun? Then welcome aboard the boomerang bus …

The boomerang is an Australian icon. It instantly conjures up images of Australia and the country's Aboriginal people. The boomerang is unique because of its capacity to return to the thrower – if thrown properly. It is traditionally used as a hunting tool, but that's probably not why you are holding one right now. More likely, you're interested in its recreational use: learning to throw it and catch it when it (hopefully!) comes back to you. Boomerang sports are becoming increasingly popular around the world, with international governing bodies and competitions being established across many continents. As an outdoor pursuit, 'boomeranging' is a healthy, wholesome way to spend an afternoon, with no need for a keyboard, controller or touch screen, and is great for general fitness, coordination and letting off steam. Best of all, boomeranging is fantastic, fast-paced, addictive and FUN!

Are you left-handed or right-handed? This makes a big difference in boomeranging. Most boomerangs are solely left- or right-handed, so you need to check what you've got. Right-handed boomerangs won't work if you throw them with your left hand, and vice versa. Luckily for you, the one that comes with this book will work with either hand. Just make sure you read page 26 if you plan to throw it with your left hand.

Boomerang background

Where did boomerangs come from? *Wherever they were thrown from! Ha, ha!* The serious answer takes us back several thousand years, to a time when shaped sticks were weapons and only some of them came back.

No one knows for sure how old boomerangs are, but some have been found to be up to ten thousand years old. Evidence of even older 'hunting sticks' has been found in Europe, and other similar sticks exist around the world. Many of these hunting sticks were shaped to make them fly accurately and fast – they may be the first examples of heavier-than-air flying machines. However, they were not designed to return to the thrower.

It is argued that these non-returning sticks should not be referred to as boomerangs. Certainly, they were aerodynamic, and designed so that they could be used for hunting when thrown properly. But Aboriginal dialects gave these sticks different names, none of which was linked to the word 'boomerang'.

The V-shaped, returning boomerang was most likely refined as hunters realised that certain shapes followed an elliptical path when they were thrown, bringing them back to their owner. This was useful when hunting birds – the sticks could be used to frighten them off course and into traps set by the hunters. It is believed that the hunters also realised what fun these boomerangs could be, and started to play with them for recreational purposes.

The naturally curved roots of mulga and wattle trees lent themselves to use as early returning boomerangs.

Early boomerangs and hunting sticks

When Captain James Cook landed in Botany Bay (in what is now Sydney, Australia), he noted that the local Aboriginals were armed with 'wooden swords' – huge, non-returning hunting sticks – and even took one back to his homeland as a souvenir.

These hunting sticks were large enough and heavy enough to stun a kangaroo when thrown accurately. But of course, no stick is going to take out such large prey and then return to its point of origin. The sticks were practical and useful tools – as Cook noted, they could be used as hand-held weapons. By banging them on the ground, or two of them together, they could serve as a musical instrument. They were handy for digging and for poking the fire.

No one can be sure exactly how returning boomerangs evolved from those original throwing sticks, but many historians feel that these changes occurred with sport in mind. Nowadays, boomerangs are so much more than 'returning sticks'. They are made of state-of-the-art materials, but their beauty still lies in their relative simplicity, low cost, and the satisfaction that comes with perfecting the art of throwing and catching them.

Boomerangs have played a constant part in Australian hunting history, possibly because they are well suited to the territory, where they are used to hunt large, easily spotted prey in wide-open country areas. The fact that boomerangs in Australia were never superseded by the bow and arrow may also contribute to their status as an Australian icon.

Hunting sticks and boomerangs have many uses, both practical and ceremonial.

Works of art

Boomerangs can be beautiful things to behold. They come in many different forms, from traditional wooden boomerangs to the flimsy, coloured thermoplastic kind. To be honest, what the latter lacks in good looks, it will probably make up in grace when you first start to throw. It's best to save the traditional kind until your skills are up to scratch.

Traditional wooden boomerangs can be bought all over Australia, as well as many other far-flung places (pardon the pun!), but you might not get a guarantee of its provenance or authenticity. Be careful when buying traditional boomerangs – they may not be the real thing.

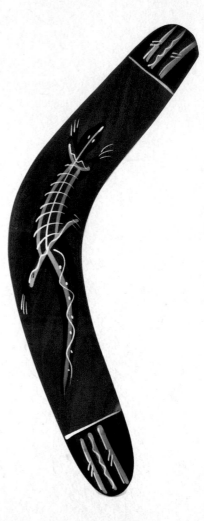

Modern designs are as varied as their creators, and come in all colours, shapes and sizes. The traditional shallow V-shape is sometimes distorted and stretched, or abandoned altogether. Two arms become three, or four, and the beautifully burned or painted wildlife images are replaced with lurid day-glo patterns.

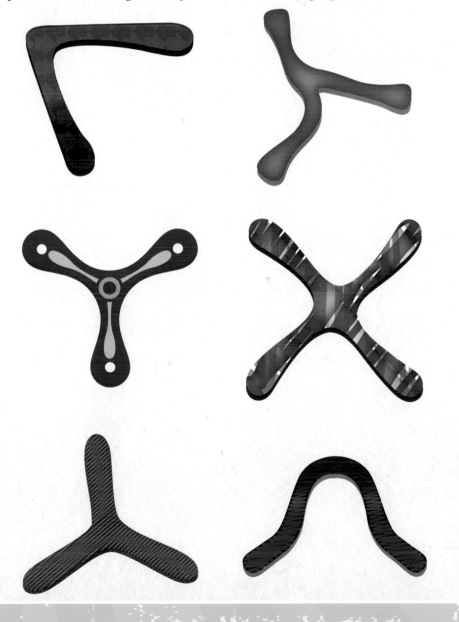

Types of boomerangs

As well as the visual differences, many other distinctions can be made between different types of boomerangs. A quick online search will produce boomerangs for beginners, boomerangs for serious competition throwers, and a multitude of styles in between. Boomerangs can be light or heavy, soft or hard, and may be designed to be thrown indoors or outdoors.

Boomerangs can even be kangaroo-shaped!

A four-armed plastic boomerang is a great place to start. These boomerangs are simple to throw, likely to come back and easy to catch.

A hat-shaped hobby boomerang needs a good strong throw, but it will travel quite a distance and come back even on a windy day.

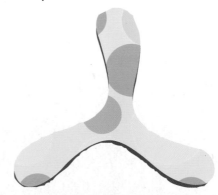

Practise indoors with a super-lightweight boomerang, which needs just a flick of the wrist to send it flying high.

As your throwing and catching skills improve, look for a carbon fibre boomerang, which is used for sports throwing.

For distance, accuracy and 'catchability' (needed in some competition events) you will welcome the long flight range of a hook boomerang.

When you reach the top of your game, you might want to try a pair of trick catch boomerangs, which need adjustments to suit your throwing style, and have extra 'hover', allowing them to be caught under your leg, behind your back, or off your feet. This trick is strictly for the experienced expert thrower.

There are even LED-lit strobe boomerangs now, for use in the dark. Gimmicky? Maybe. But they look amazing when thrown properly!

Getting started

So, now you've got the back story, you must be itching to get going. Let's start at the very beginning. These instructions are for right-handers. Turn to page 26 if you're going to be throwing left-handed.

Holding your boomerang

Grasp the right-hand end of the boomerang, with the flat face touching your palm. There are two grips you can use. The cradle grip uses your bent fingers to hold the boomerang. It's like holding a tennis racquet, or shaking hands with your boomerang. For the pinch grip, you use your thumb to grasp the boomerang against your forefinger – a bit like holding a pen. The pinch grip generally gives better spin on release, making it more likely that your boomerang will return.

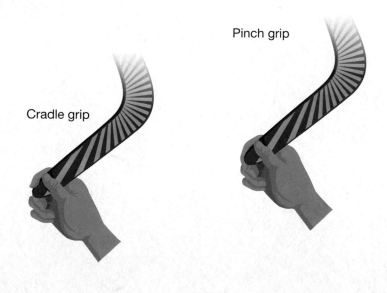

Pinch grip

Cradle grip

Get in position

When first learning to throw, make sure you give yourself plenty of room. Even the best boomerangers need a lot of space. It's important to allow for the throws to go off course without them doing any damage. Find a field or sports ground with plenty of open space.

Angling up

This is all about the angles. The most important thing to remember is that you should never throw a boomerang horizontally (like you would a frisbee). It will head straight up and come right back at you in a dangerous and unsatisfying way. You need to hold the boomerang vertically, arm raised, with it tilted ever so slightly to the right. Imagine a clock face with the boomerang tilted towards 1 o'clock.

12

1

The angle at which you hold the boomerang is called the 'layover'.

This is what happens if you throw the boomerang horizontally. Oops!

Heading in the right direction

The boomerang should be held with the V-shape pointing behind you, like this: Not like this:

Of course, if you have a three- or four-armed boomerang, that doesn't apply.

The first throw

The idea is to execute an overarm throw into the distance, at an angle of around 45 degrees from vertical – usually aiming for the treetops, if you have trees around you. Don't throw underarm – you're not skimming stones! Just imagine you're throwing a ball or serving in tennis (mimicking the motion of the racquet).

Pull back your arm so the boomerang is behind your shoulder, then swing your arm forward. Release the boomerang as your arm passes your ear, flicking your wrist as you let go. This provides the spin that makes the boomerang travel in a curve.

Using the wind

The wind plays a huge role in your throwing. Find out where it's coming from, then turn so that it's blowing onto your left cheek. With practice, you will work out how to adjust your position and the angle of your throw to account for the strength of the wind (see page 18). It's best to start on a calm day, when the wind is less than 8 km/h (5 mph).

Things to try

- Step forward with your left foot as you move into the throw.
- Throw gently but with a brisk snap, or flick of the wrist. More snap, less muscle – it works!
- Don't try to make the boomerang turn; it is designed to do that by itself.

REMEMBER: A right-handed throw will send the boomerang in an anticlockwise direction.

Don't simply let go of the boomerang; let it rip its way out of your hand.

Working with the wind

As you practise more and more, you should begin to see the different routes your boomerang can take. At worst, it will crash land and you'll have a long walk to retrieve it. At best, it will come back to you and land neatly in your hands.

In between those two outcomes, the possibilities are that it will land either too far in front or too far behind to be caught. Check out the wind conditions and see if you can make the necessary adjustments. You can turn into or away from the wind, depending on what's going wrong, or adjust your layover.

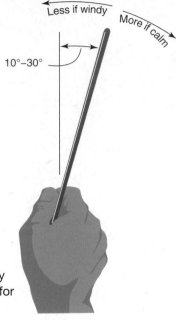

Less if windy

More if calm

10°–30°

Adjust the layover angle by a few degrees to account for the wind strength.

Stand facing the wind, and then turn 45 degrees to the right (or to the left, if you're left-handed). If there is no wind, you can throw in any direction you like.

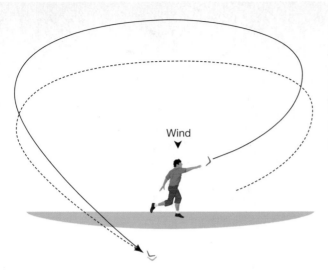

A stronger wind will often result in your boomerang landing further behind you than you are used to. Try turning away from the wind (to your right) by a few degrees.

If the wind drops, your boomerang will start to land ahead of you or to the side. Turn to the left a little (into where you judged the wind to be coming from) and throw again.

Wind

To account for a strong wind, try turning 10 degrees further, then another 10, and then another 10 if necessary.

Direction of wind

Launch direction

As wind becomes stronger

When you pick up a wayward boomerang, always return to the same starting (centre) point for each new throw. This is safest, and it will also allow you to learn to throw consistently.

Having problems?

No one said this would be easy, so persevere. Learning to throw consistently requires patience, and you may find that you've walked the equivalent of a marathon retrieving wayward boomerangs by the time your boomerang starts coming back to you. Here are a few of the things you may need to correct.

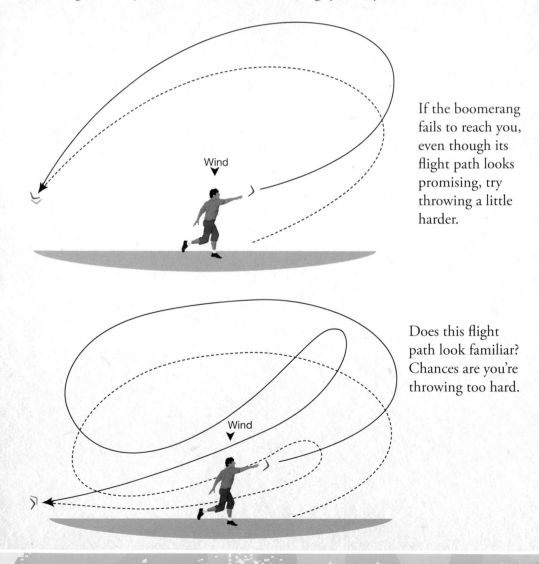

Wind

If the boomerang fails to reach you, even though its flight path looks promising, try throwing a little harder.

Wind

Does this flight path look familiar? Chances are you're throwing too hard.

As you get more accomplished at throwing, you will recognise how slight adjustments can affect the path of your boomerang. Too much layover (sidearm) produces a bad throw, but not allowing enough layover can also interrupt your boomerang's smooth flight.

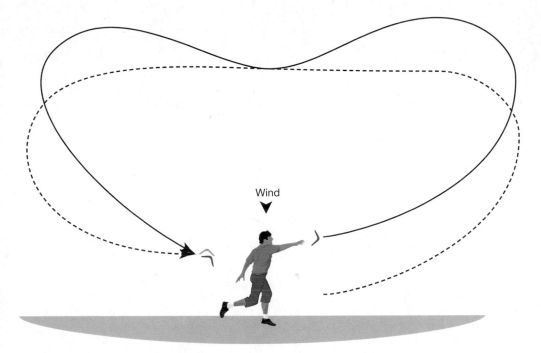

Wind

This throw didn't allow enough layover, interrupting the boomerang's smooth path.

Read more on pages 28–29 about adjusting the shape and design of your boomerang to make it fly exactly how you want it to.

Learn WELSH

What? What does speaking Welsh have to do with throwing a boomerang? Don't panic – you don't need to learn a new language in order to be able to throw. 'WELSH' is simply a mnemonic for the things you need to remember: an *aide-mémoire*, as it were. What? You don't speak French either?

W is for Wind

Come to grips with direction of the throw in relation to the wind, in order to perfect your boomeranging.

E is for Elevation

Aim for the tops of the trees! If there are no trees, try to release the boomerang at eye height.

L is for Layover

That's the technical term for the tilt of the boomerang. Remember, 1 o'clock. Too close to 3 o'clock is known as 'sidearm' and is bad for most types of throw.

S is for Spin

It's all about the spin, which comes from the snap of the wrist as you propel the boomerang forward.

H is for Hardness

As in, how hard you can throw. This isn't as important as spin, but with practice you will find out how hard you need to throw in order to achieve a good distance or travelling speed. This is more important if you want to train for competitions.

The final flourish

Okay, so you're getting good enough to throw a boomerang and have it come back to you. Now try to catch it! You can do this in a few different ways.

Two-handed catch

The best, no-frills-attached catch is using two hands. The boomerang should return to you in an almost horizontal position, allowing you to catch it safely. Clap one hand on top of it and the other beneath it, sandwiching the boomerang between your palms or your fingers.

Step 1

Step 2

WARNING! If the boomerang is travelling too fast, don't try to catch it!

Trick catches

When your success rate for catching returning boomerangs is nearly 100 per cent, you can start to show off a bit. Try catching the boomerang behind your back, or under one leg. Juggle the boomerang with your foot before catching it, or catch it with your feet. These are all recognised competition catches and each have their own name and points value (see page 42 to find out more).

If you're keen to practise trick catches, wear protective gloves. Something like cycling or weightlifting gloves will give you the grip you need while also providing padding, to cushion the blow.

Left-handed throwing

Here's the lowdown for lefties. Much of what is said on pages 14 to 25 will still apply, so don't skip that section completely. However, here's what's different.

Holding your boomerang

Grasp the left-hand end of the boomerang, with the flat face touching your palm. Choose between the cradle grip and pinch grip (see page 14) and get into position (see page 15). Just like a rightie, you're throwing upwards, but with your boomerang tilted slightly to the left – 11 o'clock instead of 1 o'clock. If you're tilting it to 9 o'clock then you're into sidearm territory.

Into the wind

Once you've figured out where the wind is coming from, you need to turn in the opposite direction to a right-handed thrower, so the wind is blowing onto your right cheek. This will involve turning about 45 degrees to your left. Your first throw should be as described on page 17, but you will step forward with your right foot, rather than your left.

Troubleshooting

If the wind speed is affecting your throws, you need to make the same adjustments as a right-hander, but your turns will be in the opposite direction. They will still follow the same principles, however. So, if your boomerang is landing too far behind you, you still turn away from the wind. It's just that this will involve a left turn, rather than a right.

REMEMBER: A left-handed throw will send the boomerang in a clockwise direction.

Fine tuning

As well as fine tuning your throwing technique, you can also make adjustments to the boomerang itself. Some boomerangs are made of materials that allow you to bend the tips, and weights can also be added to alter a boomerang's flying properties. Putting rubber bands on the boomerang will also change its flight. This can help in very windy conditions.

For a boomerang that climbs too high too quickly, bend the tips down slightly. Start with the leading edge and see if that helps. Make sure you only tweak it, to ensure that you don't break the boomerang.

Bend one or both tips upwards if your boomerang persists in dipping down long before it starts heading back to you.

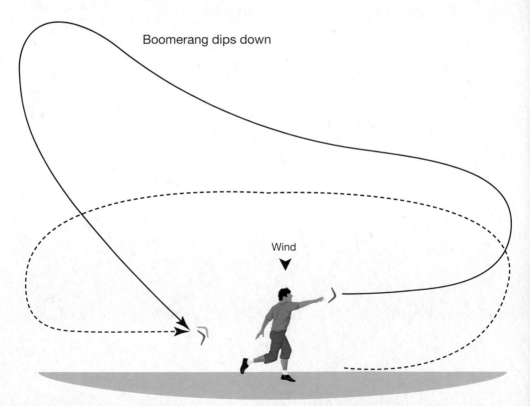

Boomerang dips down

Wind

Problem solved!

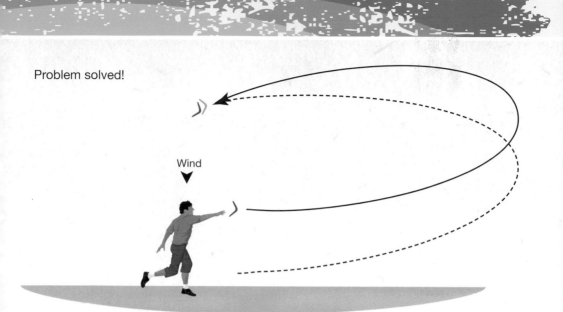

Wind

Don't worry about fine-tuning your boomerang until your throws are fairly consistent. If your throws are still inconsistent, you won't be able to judge whether the boomerang flies differently because you tuned it, or just because you threw it differently.

Why does a boomerang fly?

Because it's clever! Oh wait – you actually want to know? Oh, okay then …

A boomerang has two wings, which are shaped just like aeroplane wings. That's an aerofoil shape: rounded on one side and flat on the other. This shape rearranges the airflow, causing a difference in air pressure that keeps the wing aloft. This gives the boomerang lift, which is what keeps it up in the air.

Trailing edge   Leading edge
          Cross-section

This cross-section shows how the top side of a boomerang is rounded, and the bottom is flat.

However, the multiple-winged design of a boomerang makes it more like a propeller than a set of aeroplane wings. It literally spins as it flies through the air. Each wing, or aerofoil, has a leading edge, and they are positioned in such a way that as the boomerang turns, there is always a leading edge facing in the direction of flight.

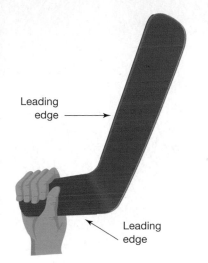

Leading edge →

Leading edge →

A left-handed boomerang.

A left-handed boomerang is designed in the opposite way to a right-handed one, so that the leading edge is on the other side.

Why does a boomerang come back?

When you throw the boomerang, you send it forwards, but with a spinning motion. That spinning motion gives the top wing (which is rotating in the direction of flight) a higher airspeed than the other wing (which is rotating against the direction of flight).

This difference in airspeed generates uneven lift, which tries to tip the boomerang over. The 'tipping effect' of the uneven lift causes the boomerang's flight path to curve. It's just like when you ride a bicycle with no hands, and lean over to make it turn.

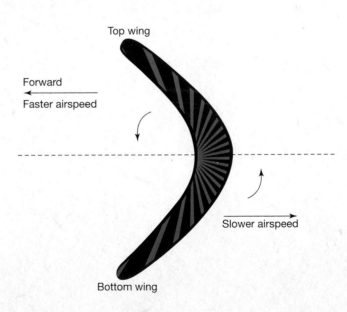

Top wing

Forward
Faster airspeed

Slower airspeed

Bottom wing

'My boomerang doesn't work!'

This is a common complaint among first-time throwers. Rest assured, it does work. It's just that you're not quite throwing it correctly. No commercially available boomerang should fail to fly if it is handled properly. Re-read the instructions on pages 14–20 and try again, making small adjustments until you achieve that mind-blowing, spirit-soaring feeling that comes with throwing a boomerang and seeing it head back in your direction.

Recreational boomeranging

The ancient boomerang was used for hunting, as a musical instrument and for digging. The modern boomerang is used purely for fun, fitness and, for a few fanatics, for competitions.

Learning to throw a boomerang is like starting a new gym class. Your fitness will definitely improve, thanks to all the running and retrieving involved while you're learning. Even though power and strength aren't needed to make the boomerang fly, you will probably still find that your throwing arm aches at first, simply because it's been performing an unusual action over and over again.

Boomerang throwing is a social activity. When you're just starting out, people may offer advice (ask to see them throw before you believe a word of it!). As you get better at it, they'll just want to chat and soak up your expertise by observing your skills in action.

You might want to seek out like-minded individuals. Currently, more than a dozen countries have a national boomerang team and a national association, where you can find out more about local events and organisations. The USA and Germany in particular take their boomeranging very seriously, and the world team championships are held every two years in locations all around the world.

Boomeranging has also become a form of performance art. Supremely skilled throwers can bang a gong, blow out a candle, burst a balloon and perform all sorts of other tricks with their boomerangs.

Be a sport

Competitive boomerang throwing is a serious business, with its own governing bodies and rule books. There are six main events and all manner of amazing records that have been set.

Some boomerang throwing events require a marked-out field. The 20-metre (65-foot) line shows where the boomerang must travel to before it begins its return. The outer circle marks the furthest distance that the boomerang can travel. This circle may be marked at 50 metres (164 feet) or 100 metres (328 feet), depending on the event.

The other long-distance circles are used for measuring the Aussie Round, and the 2- to 10-metre (6- to 32-foot) circles are to judge the accuracy of the boomerang's return.

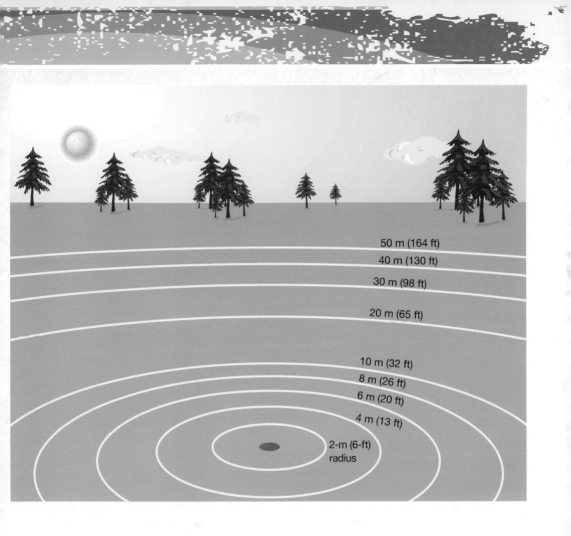

50 m (164 ft)

40 m (130 ft)

30 m (98 ft)

20 m (65 ft)

10 m (32 ft)

8 m (26 ft)

6 m (20 ft)

4 m (13 ft)

2-m (6-ft)
radius

Aussie Round

The blue-ribbon event has to be Aussie Round. This is a test of all the main skills involved in boomeranging – distance, accuracy and catching – all at once. The thrower stands in the bullseye of the measuring area and throws five times. Points are given for distance travelled, how accurately the boomerang returns, and for catching the returning boomerang.

Points for distance are only awarded if the throw accurately returns to the thrower and is caught. The top score is 6 points for a throw over 50 metres (164 feet), and another 4 points if the boomerang is caught within the 2-metre (6-foot) circle.

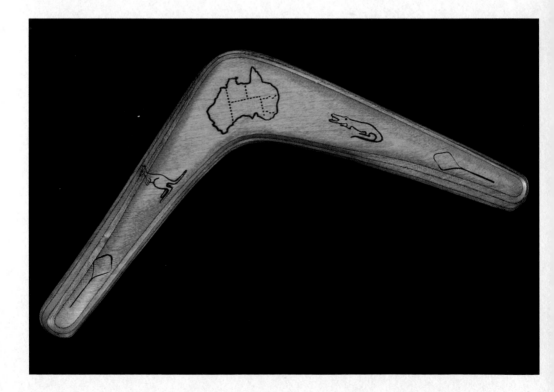

Accuracy

Accuracy events also use the bullseye, with points awarded for how close to the bullseye the boomerang returns on each of five throws. The top score is 50 points, which is awarded for five throws that all land inside the bullseye. Points are scored if the boomerang comes to rest anywhere within the 10-metre (32-foot) circle. No catching allowed!

Accuracy can be a team event, as can the Aussie Round, with four throwers on each team.

Maximum points are achieved for getting the boomerang to land in the bullseye.

Maximum Time Aloft (MTA)

MTA is short for maximum time aloft. This event uses a very specific type of boomerang that has one arm longer than the other. This makes it hover more than other boomerangs, allowing it to stay in the air for as long as possible. It needs to be thrown extremely hard!

Think you can do it? You're aiming for over a minute and a half if you want to get into the record books.

Fast Catch

The Fast Catch is a timed event where one boomerang must be thrown and caught five times. The shortest time wins. The aim is to complete all five throws and catches in under 15 seconds. Better get a move on …

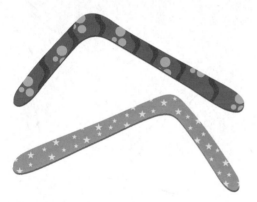

If stamina is your thing, take a closer look at the Fast Catch Endurance event. It's a test of how many fast catch throws you can achieve in five minutes. If you can't manage more than 20, then you may as well sit this one out. The world record is more than 80 catches – that's one catch every three or four seconds!

'Skying' your boomerang means losing it. Some MTA boomerangs fly too far and come down where the thrower can't see them!

A boomeranger from Ohio once caught an MTA boomerang 17 minutes after throwing it!

Doubling and Juggling

If all that simply isn't challenging enough for you, then maybe the extra buzz of throwing two boomerangs at once will appeal to your sense of showmanship?

Doubling is exactly that – throwing two boomerangs at once. Each boomerang is a different type: one has a longer flight and a shorter hover, the other has a shorter flight and a longer hover. Competitors hold both boomerangs in the same hand and throw them together. Then they have to catch them both. Easy …

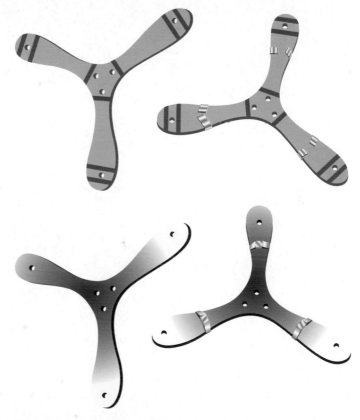

Juggling is a different discipline but still uses two boomerangs. The aim is to keep one boomerang in the air at all times. Throw and catch, throw and catch, throw and catch, until you drop one or run out of steam. The record is an incredible 555 catches set by Frenchman Yannick Charles. No problem, right?

Doublers often attach weights to one of the boomerangs to bring it down faster than the other.

Trick Catch

Here's another spectacular showy-offy event. Trick Catch involves a set of ten compulsory catches, to be performed in order of difficulty. If you make it through the first round then you have to do it all again, but this time while Doubling, using a specified pair of catches for each throw. Absolutely amazing.

Here are your ten catches, if you're feeling brave:

- left-hand catch
- right-hand catch
- behind the back
- under the leg
- eagle catch
- hackey catch
- tunnel catch
- one hand behind the back
- one hand under the leg
- foot/leg catch.

An eagle catch is one made from above the boomerang, using just one hand.

A hackey catch involves kicking the boomerang up then catching it with your hands.

For a tunnel catch, both feet must be on the ground, with one hand passing between your legs to grab the boomerang.

Both feet may be used to trap the boomerang for a foot catch.

Playing it safe

By now it should be obvious that a boomerang, if wrongly thrown, can cause harm. Be sure to follow these safety guidelines, and think before you throw.

Throw your boomerang in a safe place.

This means checking, before you let go, that there is plenty of room for the boomerang to fly, bounce or crash land without the chance of it hitting anyone or damaging anything.

Keep your distance.

Aim for a clear space of 30 metres (100 feet) in all directions. Better still, practise on an empty sports field.

Stay alert and be prepared to shout a warning.

If you see someone in the line of fire, shout. Quickly. And LOUDLY.

Don't throw a boomerang like a frisbee.

If you throw it flat, it will swoop and dive dangerously and unpredictably. A boomerang should be thrown in an almost vertical position.

Do not leave children unsupervised while you throw.

Spectators are constantly at risk of losing sight of the flying boomerang. Remember, these things were used to stun large prey animals. They're not supposed to catch offspring and siblings!

Only throw one boomerang at a time.

Some sports competitions involve throwing two boomerangs simultaneously. Leave that for the experts!

Don't throw too hard.

At least, not while you're learning. Even a half-powered throw should get the boomerang back to you.

Remember, it's a hobby.

That means you're doing it for fun, so it shouldn't be dangerous. It also means that you should leave competition boomerangs for the experts. They fly further and stay in the air for longer, and you need experience in order to control them.

Here's a handy hint: make your boomerang bright and bold! The easier it is to see, the less likely it is that someone will get hit by it.

Totally hooked

So there it is – just about everything you could want to know when you're starting out. At least, everything you can get from reading a book. Now what you really need to do is get out there and try it for yourself.

A word of warning: be prepared to be gripped by boomerang fever. Common symptoms include severe muscle pain in one arm, grazes and scratches (from retrieving your boomerang from inaccessible locations), and raised blood pressure because you can't get the blasted thing to do what you want it to! But it really is worth it for that exciting moment when you release the boomerang and watch it spin a beautiful, elliptical path back towards you. That's something that words can't describe: you need to experience it for yourself.

So what are you waiting for? Off you throw!

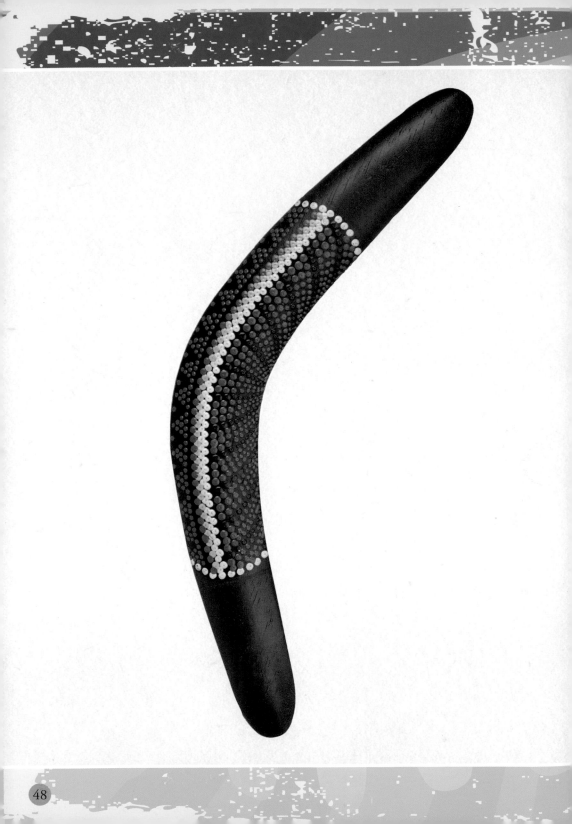